FUN FACT FILE: SPACE!

20 FUN FACTS ABOUT GALAXIES

By Michael Sabatino

Gareth Stevens PUBLISHING

Please visit our website, www.garethstevens.com. For a free color catalog of all our high-quality books, call toll free 1-800-542-2595 or fax 1-877-542-2596.

Library of Congress Cataloging-in-Publication Data

Sabatino, Michael.
20 fun facts about galaxies / by Michael Sabatino.
p. cm. — (Fun fact file: space!)
Includes index.
ISBN 978-1-4824-0997-0 (pbk.)
ISBN 978-1-4824-0998-7 (6-pack)
ISBN 978-1-4824-0996-3 (library binding)
1. Galaxies — Juvenile literature. I. Sabatino, Michael. II. Title.
QB857.3 S23 2014
523.1—d23

First Edition

Published in 2015 by
Gareth Stevens Publishing
111 East 14th Street, Suite 349
New York, NY 10003

Designer: Sarah Liddell
Editor: Greg Roza

Photo credits: Cover, p. 1 Vadim Sadovski/Shutterstock.com; p. 5 Giovanni Benintende/Shutterstock.com; p. 6 photo courtesy of NASA; ESA; G. Illingworth, D. Magee, and P. Oesch, University of California, Santa Cruz; R. Bouwens, Leiden University; and the HUDF09 Team; p. 7 Thunderf00t/Wikimedia Commons; p. 8 Stocktrek Images/Stocktrek Images/Getty images; p. 9 Bill Frische/Shutterstock.com; p. 10 Mprach/Wikimedia Commons; p. 11 photo courtesy of European Southern Observatory (ESO)/Wikimedia Commons; p. 12 Atlas Image courtesy of 2MASS/UMASS/IPAC-Caltech/NASA/NSF; p. 13 Nrisinger/Wikimedia Commons; p. 14 CGruda/Wikimedia Commons; p. 15 Handout/Handout/Getty Images News/Getty Images; p. 16 Stocktrek Images/Stocktrek Images/Getty Images; p. 17 Lonely/Shutterstock.com; p. 18 Hallowedland/Shutterstock.com; p. 19 NASA NASA/Photo Researchers/Getty Images; p. 21 (IC 1101) NASA/CXC/UCI/A. Lewis et al./Wikimedia Commons; p. 21 (Andromeda) Igor Chekalin/Shutterstock.com; p. 21 (Milky Way) Lev Savitskiy/Shutterstock.com; p. 22 Reinhold Wittich/Stocktrek Images/Stocktrek Images/Getty Images; p. 23 Stocktrek Images/Stocktrek Images/Getty Images; p. 24 photo courtesy of NASA, ESA, and J. Lotz, M. Mountain, A. Koekemoer, and the HFF Team (STScI)/Wikimedia Commons; p. 25 BSIP/Contributor/Universal Images Group/Getty Images; p. 26 photo courtesy of NASA, ESA, and E. Hallman (University of Colorado, Boulder); p. 27 Mopic/Shutterstock.com; p. 29 Kevin Key/Shutterstock.com.

Printed in the United States of America

CPSIA compliance information: Batch #CS15GS: For further information contact Gareth Stevens, New York, New York at 1-800-542-2595.

Contents

Words in the glossary appear in **bold** type the first time they are used in the text.

If you found yourself under a clear sky at night, you could be lucky enough to see the Andromeda galaxy, which is a galaxy very far away from ours. Galaxies are huge groups of stars, dust, and gas. They come in lots of different shapes and sizes.

There once was a time when scientists thought that our own Milky Way galaxy was all there was to the entire **universe**. However, with the help of powerful telescopes, we now know there are billions of other galaxies beyond our own!

The Andromeda galaxy, our biggest galactic neighbor, appears several times wider than a full moon in the sky.

FACT 1

There are so many galaxies in the universe we can't possibly count them all.

In recent years, **astronomers** have used the powerful Hubble Space Telescope to take pictures of deep space. They found thousands of galaxies never seen before. Using pictures like this, scientists estimate there are about 100 billion to 200 billion galaxies in the universe!

This is just one small fraction of the universe. Most of these bright spots aren't stars—they're entire galaxies!

FACT 2

Stars in distant galaxies are like measuring sticks that show how far away they are.

Astronomers have discovered that certain types of stars shine in a **predictable** way. Measuring how bright or dim these types of stars are reveals their distance from us. However, some galaxies are too far away to see individual stars.

This exploding star, called a supernova, gives scientists an idea of how far the host galaxy is from us.

FACT 3

Galaxies have three main shapes.

There are three types of galaxies—spiral, elliptical, and irregular. Spiral galaxies, like the Milky Way, are flat. Elliptical galaxies are round like a ball or oval like an egg. Irregular galaxies have very odd shapes caused by the **gravity** of other nearby galaxies.

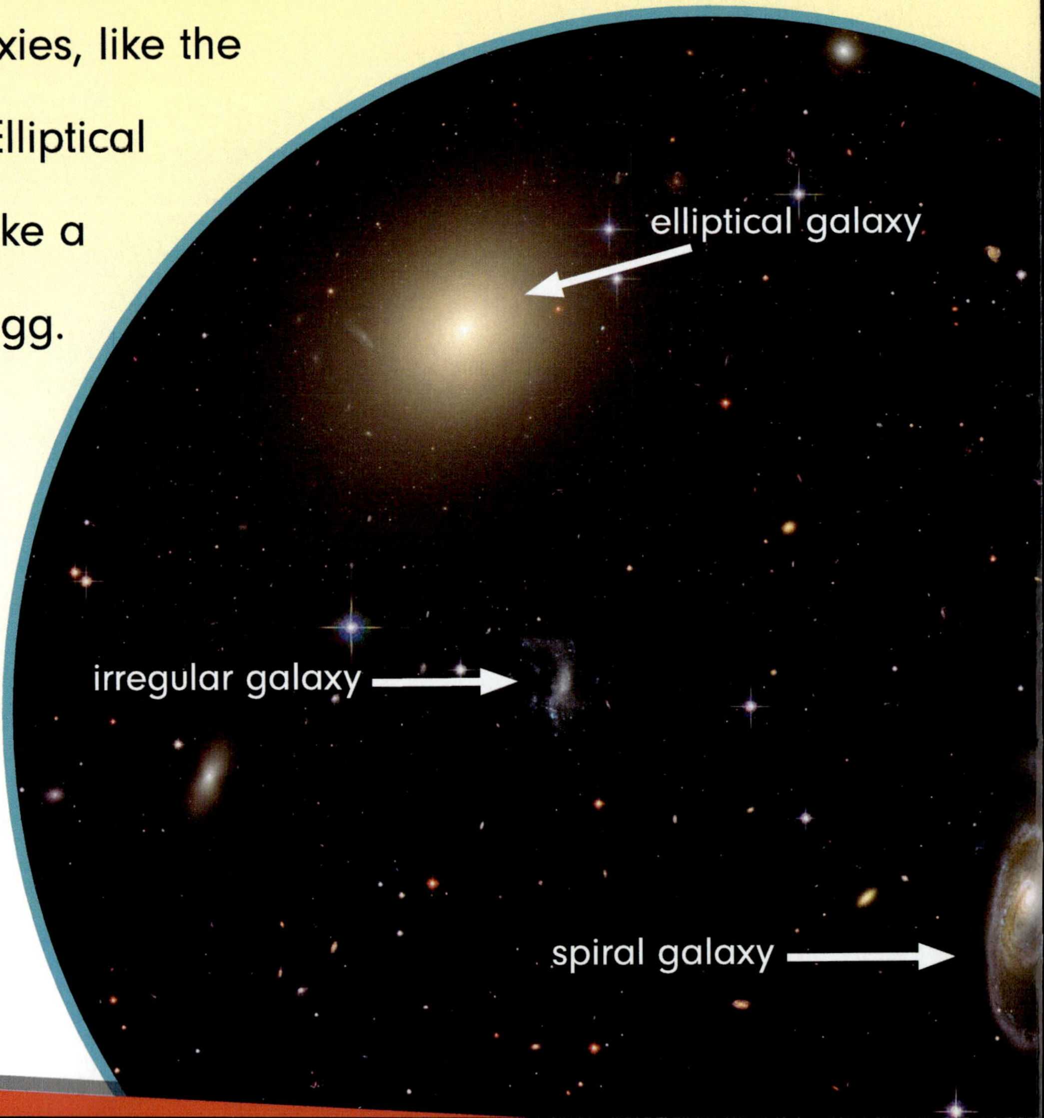

Galaxy collisions can make all sorts of beautiful shapes.

FACT 4

There's a lot of space between most galaxies, but they sometimes crash into each other.

Galaxies can run into each other when their gravity pulls them together. These **collisions** can take hundreds of millions of years to play out. If it happens just the right way, two galaxies can join together to form a single, bigger galaxy.

FACT 5

The Milky Way is downright huge!

The Milky Way is about 100,000 **light-years** wide. To give you an idea of how far that is, it takes light 100,000 years to make its way from one side of our galaxy to the other. And light travels at 671 million miles (1.08 billion km) per hour!

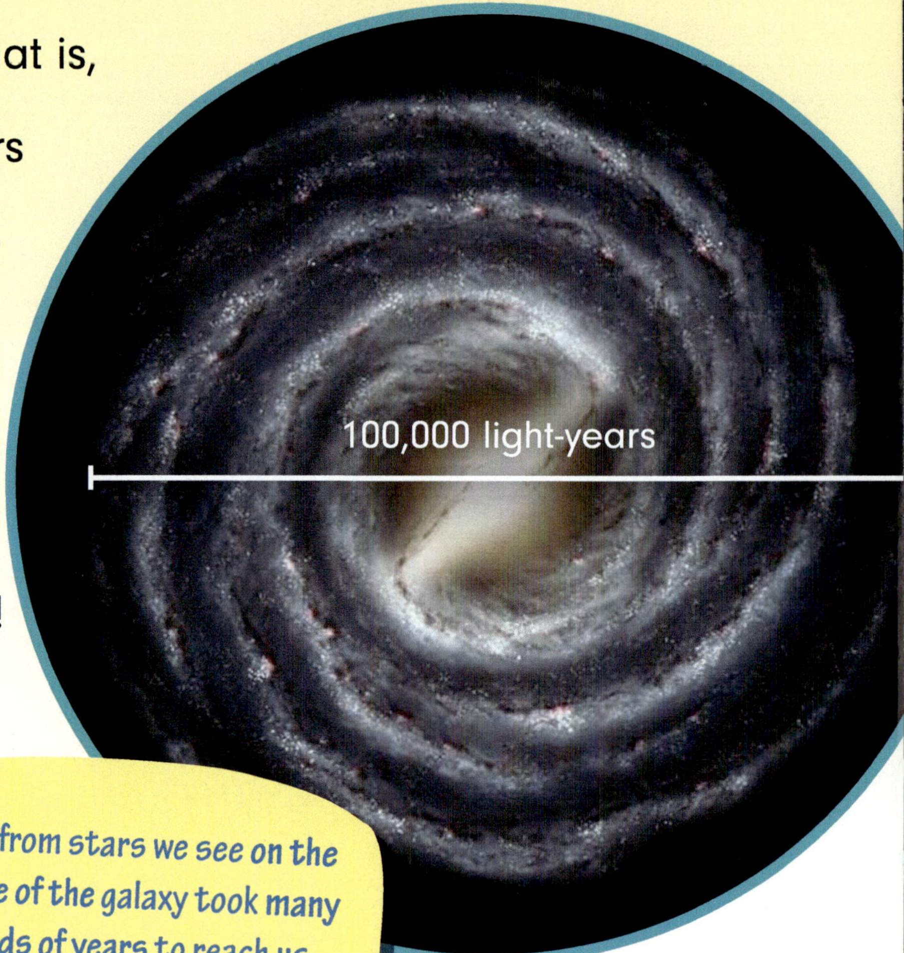

The light from stars we see on the other side of the galaxy took many thousands of years to reach us.

1 million = 1,000,000
1 billion = 1,000,000,000
1 trillion = 1,000,000,000,000

The galaxy named NGC 6872 is one of the largest galaxies found so far. It's about five times the size of the Milky Way galaxy.

FACT 6

The Milky Way galaxy might be huge, but some galaxies make it seem tiny.

The Milky Way has about 300 billion stars, including our sun. This means it's a pretty average-sized galaxy. Some galaxies can have as few as 100 million stars. Then there are the real monster galaxies that have as many as 100 trillion stars!

Exploring the Milky Way

The Milky Way is a spiral galaxy. Here are two different views of what it probably looks like.

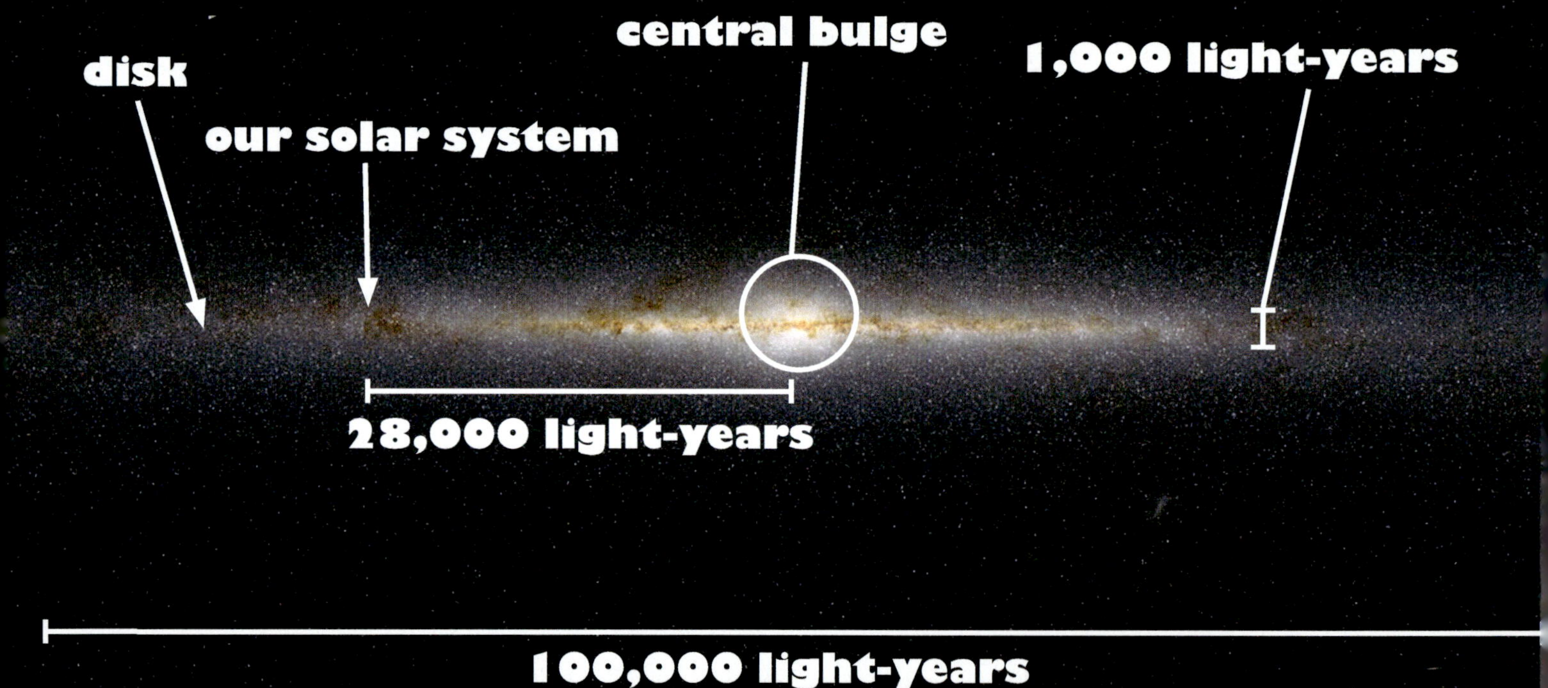

100,000 light-years
our solar system
central bulge

This is what the night sky could look like in 3.75 billion years as Andromeda approaches the Milky Way.

FACT 7

Our galaxy is on a collision course with the Andromeda galaxy.

Andromeda is headed straight for us at 250,000 miles (402,336 km) per hour! Even at that rate, it'll take about 4 billion years before it reaches us. When it's all over, the two galaxies will have joined together to form a single giant elliptical galaxy.

FACT 8

Scientists think there are many other Earthlike planets in the Milky Way.

Recent studies suggest there could be as many as 40 billion Earthlike planets in our Milky Way galaxy alone. Since there are 100 billion to 200 billion other galaxies out there, the chances seem pretty good that there's another planet somewhere in the universe that also has life on it.

There are planets that orbit their stars in the "goldilocks zone." This is where the temperature is just right for water to exist.

FACT 9

Galaxies are mostly empty space.

As big as galaxies are, they're made up mostly of empty space. That's because the stars inside them are so far apart. In fact, when the Milky Way collides with Andromeda, the chance of another star hitting our sun is almost zero.

Though star collisions are rare, galactic mergers create new stars when their gas and dust mix together. A galactic merger is when galaxies come together by gravity and form a single larger galaxy.

"Massive" means very large, so "supermassive" describes something unbelievably large. The supermassive black hole at the center of the Milky Way is 10 times the size of the sun and has 4 million times the mass.

FACT 10

Galaxies are home to the most destructive force in the universe—black holes.

Scientists think nearly all galaxies have a supermassive **black hole** at their center. These are much larger than normal black holes. Some have billions of times the mass of our sun! Instead of falling into the black hole, most of the stars in a galaxy orbit around it.

FACT 11

Some galaxies are home to the brightest objects in the universe—quasars.

Some supermassive black holes gobble up nearby matter so quickly they become quasars. They glow brighter as they suck in more and more matter. The firestorm of activity is so intense that it seems to outshine the rest of the galaxy that surrounds it.

This quasar has so much energy that matter is getting blown 100,000 light-years away from it!

Dark matter, in blue, is detected as two galaxy clusters merge together.

FACT 12

Galaxies are packed full of a mysterious substance called dark matter.

Scientists found that galaxies spin so fast they should fly apart, but they don't! Some mysterious substance is keeping them together with its gravity. This so-called dark matter has scientists stumped. It can't be directly seen, but it's keeping our Milky Way from spiraling apart.

FACT 13

Dark energy is causing distant galaxies to drift away from us.

A force called dark energy is causing the universe to **expand**. This means that all distant galaxies appear to be moving away from us. About 2 trillion years from now, these galaxies will fade from view and disappear forever.

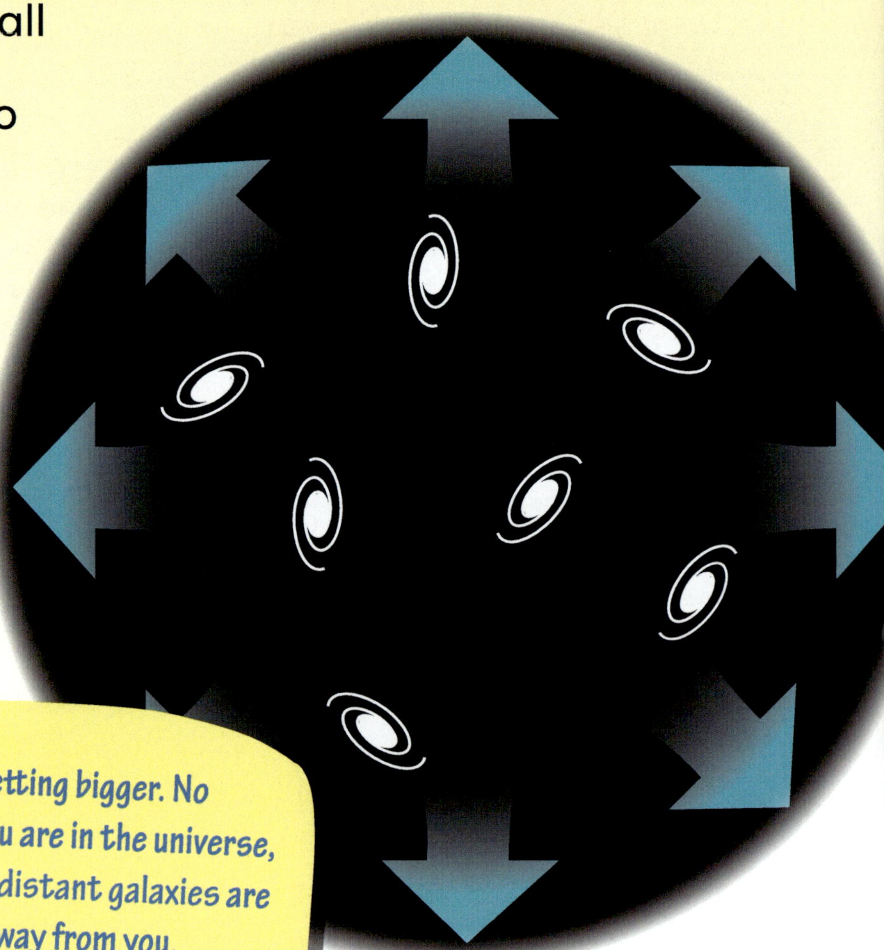

Space is getting bigger. No matter where you are in the universe, it appears that distant galaxies are floating away from you.

Intergalactic Family

FACT 14

The largest known galaxy is about 60 times bigger than the Milky Way.

So, what's the largest galaxy we've ever seen? That would be galaxy IC 1101. At about 6 million light-years across, it has over 100 trillion stars. It's big enough to **engulf** the Milky Way and reach out well past our neighboring galaxy, Andromeda!

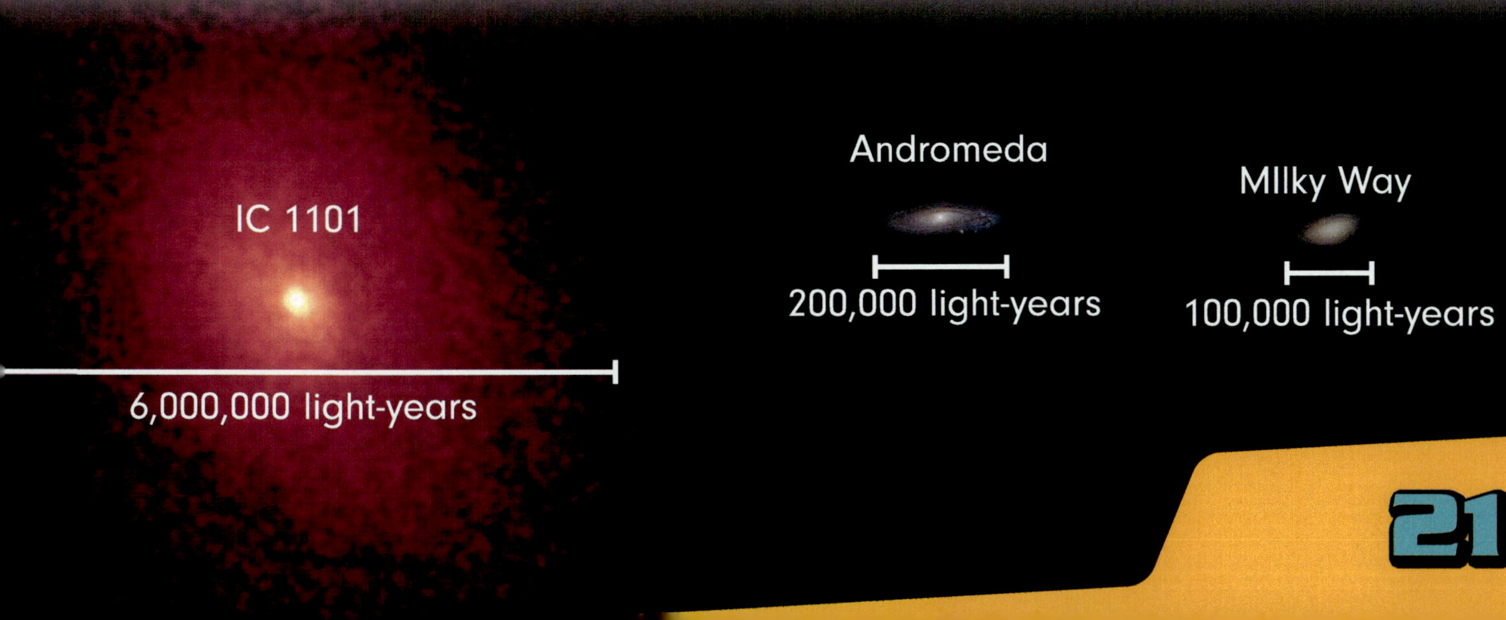

FACT 15

Galaxies gather together in clusters.

Galaxies are made of gas, dust, and stars grouped together. But even galaxies themselves are grouped together. The Milky Way is one of about 30 galaxies in what's called the Local Group. These other galaxies are within about 4 million light-years of our own galaxy.

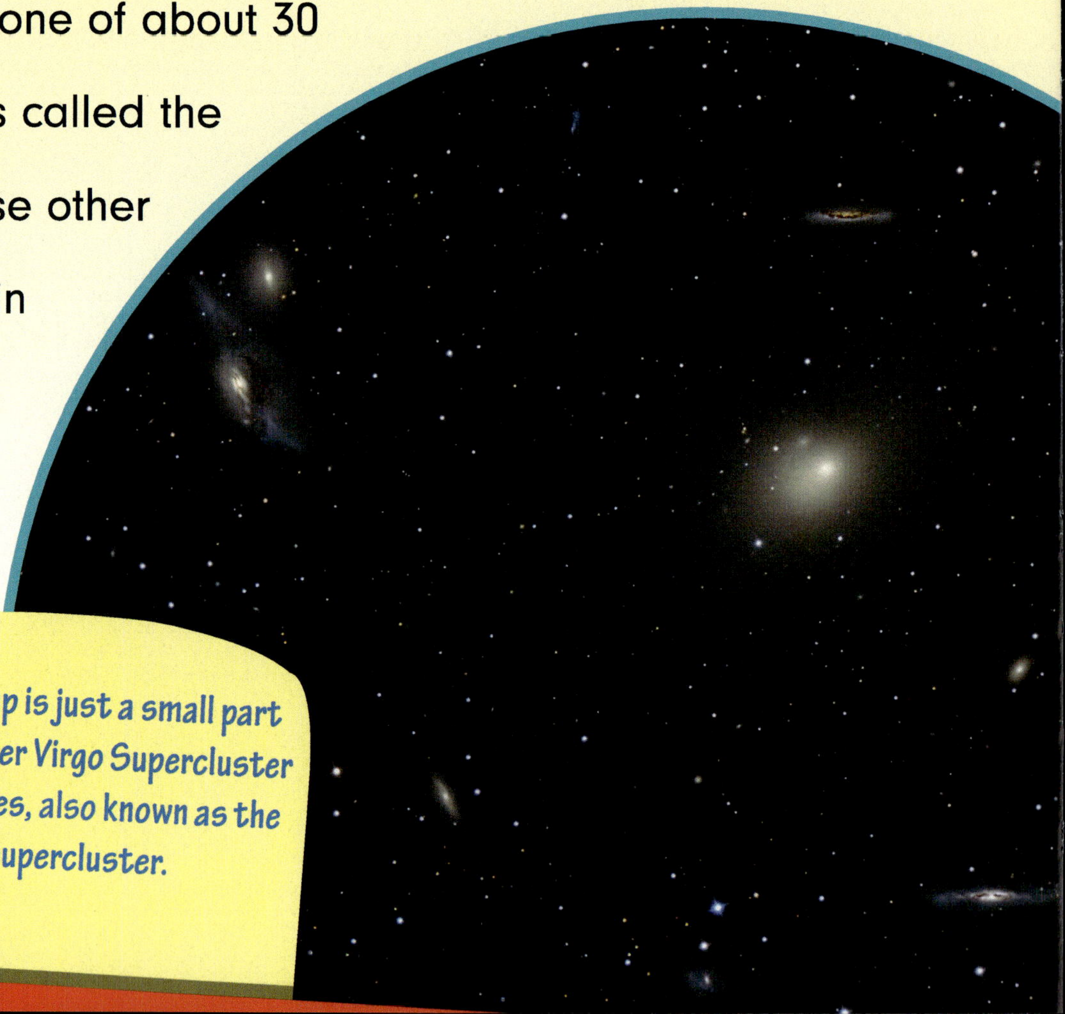

The Local Group is just a small part of the even bigger Virgo Supercluster group of galaxies, also known as the Local Supercluster.

Galaxy clusters like the Perseus Cluster are incredibly huge objects grouped together by their own gravity.

FACT 16

A recent discovery found the biggest thing in the universe—and it's made of galaxies.

Scientists recently discovered the single largest structure in the known universe. The Hercules–Corona Borealis Great Wall is a group of quasar galaxies drawn together by their own gravity. It measures 10 billion light-years across, which is more than twice the size of the previous record holder.

FACT 17

The first galaxies formed over 13 billion years ago.

With the help of a special telescope, astronomers recently discovered the oldest and most distant galaxy ever detected. It formed just 700 million years after the Big Bang—the event scientists believe created the universe. The universe was still very "young" when the first galaxies appeared.

This photograph, taken by the Hubble Space Telescope, shows a giant galaxy cluster in deep space.

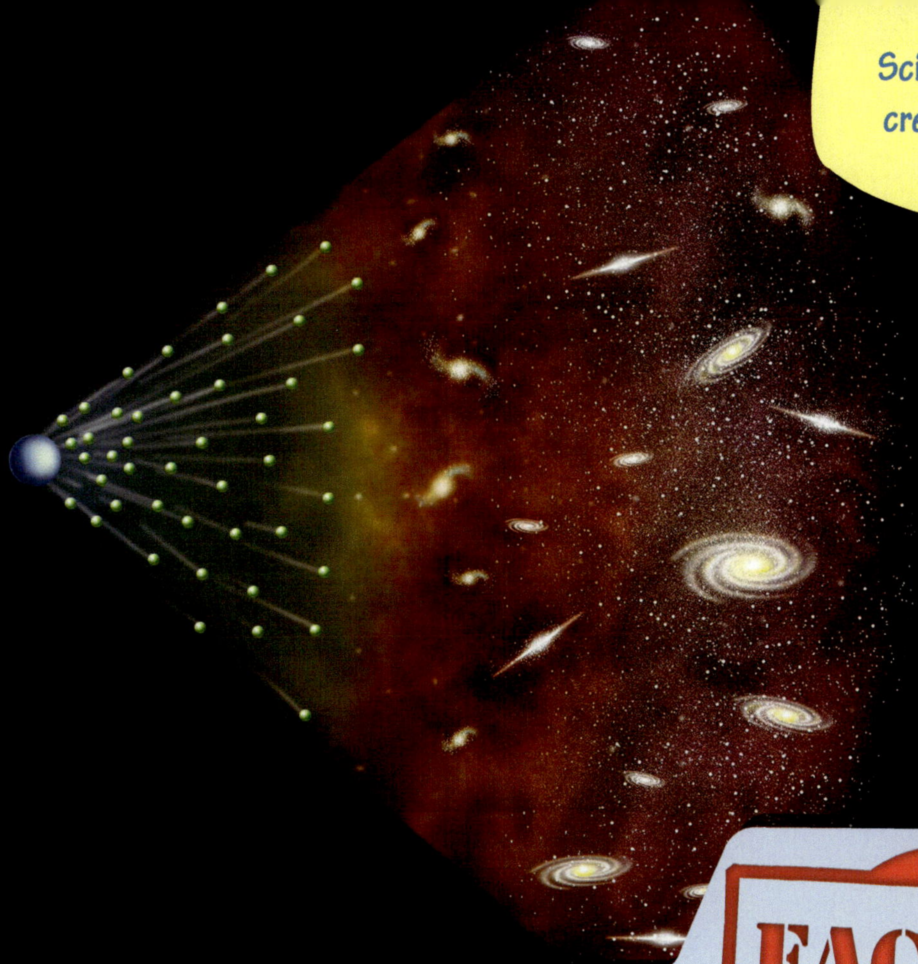

Scientists believe hydrogen was created within the first second after the Big Bang.

FACT 18

The seeds of galaxies were planted before the universe was 1 second old.

Scientists believe the universe began about 13.7 billion years ago. It was an extremely small, hot bubble that expanded and cooled to what we see today.

FACT 19

A vast web of galaxies stretches across the entire known universe.

Clusters of galaxies form a **cosmic** web that spreads throughout the entire universe. The thin bands—or filaments—of this web are separated by vast areas of empty space. If we could look at the universe from far away, this is what it would look like.

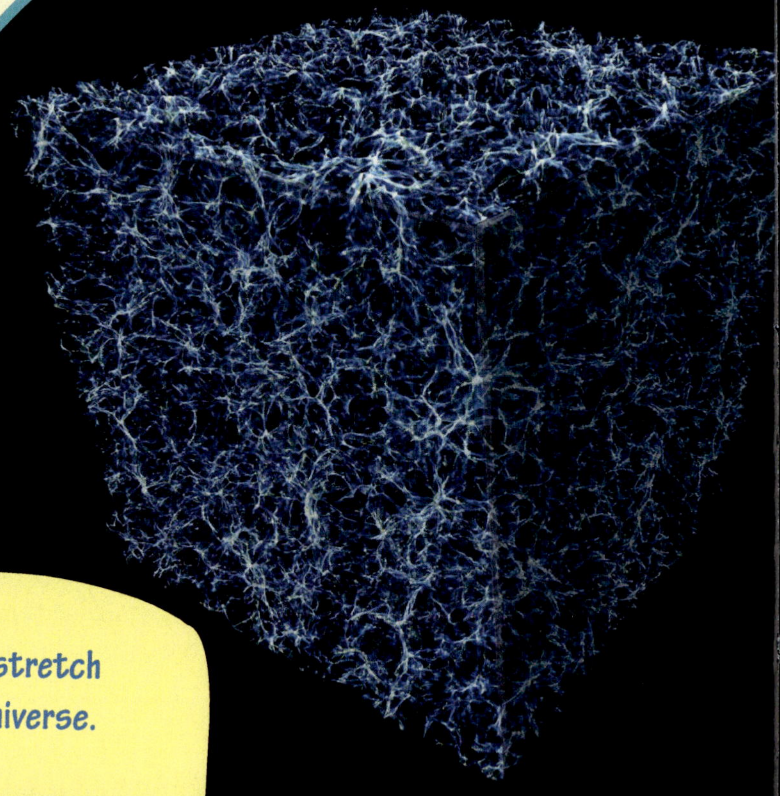

Galactic filaments stretch across the whole universe.

Modern scientific theory says that black holes will eventually lose all their mass over the course of their lifetime.

FACT 20

Galaxies will eventually fade into nothing.

Billions of years from now, after star formation stops, gravitational forces will cause stars to fly out of their home galaxies. Any stars that remain will fall into their galaxy's supermassive black hole. The remaining supermassive black holes will eventually **evaporate** and disappear forever.

Knowing Our Place

From ancient ellipticals to swirling spirals, each galaxy is **unique**. They have helped us understand where we came from and where we're going. In the span of 100 years, our knowledge of the universe has grown considerably.

We once thought the Milky Way was the only galaxy in the universe. We now know the Milky Way is just a tiny piece of the vast web of galaxies strung across the **cosmos**. Imagine what we'll know in another 100 years!

This is our view from inside the Milky Way. The faint, cloudy band of light is our own galaxy as we see it from Earth.

Glossary

astronomer: a person who studies stars, planets, and other heavenly bodies

black hole: an object with gravity so strong that nothing can escape it if it gets too close, not even light

collision: an event where two or more objects crash into each other

cosmic: relating to the universe outside of Earth

cosmos: the universe, or everything that exists

engulf: to swallow up

evaporate: to fade away

expand: to grow bigger in size

gravity: the force that pulls objects toward the center of a planet or star

light-year: the distance light travels in 1 year, or about 5.9 trillion miles (9.5 trillion km)

predictable: expected or known beforehand

unique: one of a kind

universe: everything that exists

For More Information

Books

Aguilar, David. *Planets, Stars, and Galaxies: A Visual Encyclopedia of Our Universe.* Washington, DC: National Geographic, 2007.

Kerrod, Robin. *Universe.* New York, NY: DK Publishing, 2009.

Websites

Interactive Map of the Milky Way Galaxy
workshop.chromeexperiments.com/stars/
Use this interactive map to explore the Milky Way.

The Scale of the Universe 2
htwins.net/scale2/
This interactive website gives you an idea of how big the universe really is.

Solar System Matchup
science.discovery.com/video-topics/space-videos/space-school-milky-way.htm
Watch a fascinating video about the Milky Way and what it would be like to explore it.

Publisher's note to educators and parents: Our editors have carefully reviewed these websites to ensure that they are suitable for students. Many websites change frequently, however, and we cannot guarantee that a site's future contents will continue to meet our high standards of quality and educational value. Be advised that students should be closely supervised whenever they access the Internet.

Index